Date: 8/15/12

The STRANGEST Plants on Earth

GIANT PLANTS

Margee Gould

PowerKiDS
press

New York

Published in 2012 by The Rosen Publishing Group, Inc.
29 East 21st Street, New York, NY 10010

First Edition

Editor: Jennifer Way
Book Design: Ashley Drago

Photo Credits: Cover, pp. 7, 8–9, 14, 15 (right), 21 (left) Shutterstock.com; p. 4 © www.iStockphoto.com/Jeff Hathaway; p. 5 © www.iStockphoto.com/Heather Faye Bath; pp. 6, 13 iStockphoto/Thinkstock; p. 10 Renaud Visage/Getty Images; p. 11 Damien Meyer/AFP/Getty Images; p. 12 Paul Zahl/National Geographic/Getty Images; p. 15 (left) Eastcott Momatiuk/Getty Images; p. 16 (left) © Heuclin Daniel/age fotostock; p. 16 (right) Henning Kaiser/AFP/Getty Images; p. 17 © A. Jagel/age fotostock; p. 18 Jason Edwards/ Getty Images; p. 19 Tim Phillips Photos/Getty Images; p. 20 © www.iStockphoto.com/ Dejan Suc; p. 21 (right) © www.iStockphoto.com/Tony Oquias.

Library of Congress Cataloging-in-Publication Data

Gould, Margee.
 Giant plants / by Margee Gould. — 1st ed.
    p. cm. — (The strangest plants on Earth)
 Includes index.
 ISBN 978-1-4488-4990-1 (library binding)
 1. Plant size—Juvenile literature. 2. Trees—Juvenile literature. I. Title. II. Series: Strangest plants on Earth.
 QK641.G685 2012
 580—dc22
                                        2010052217

Manufactured in the United States of America

CPSIA Compliance Information: Batch #WS11PK: For Further Information contact Rosen Publishing, New York, New York at 1-800-237-9932

Contents

Giant Plants

If you have ever seen a California redwood, then you know that some plants can grow to be quite large. California redwoods grow to be more than 300 feet (91 m) tall, or about the height of a 30-floor skyscraper. That is a pretty big plant!

Not every giant, or large, plant is tall, though. Some have big flowers, some have tall trunks, and others have big smells. Some plants make clones, or exact copies of themselves, until they take up acres (ha) of land. All of these are strange and giant plants.

Above: *Rafflesia arnoldii* is the world's largest flower.

Big Life

Plants need food and water to live. Most plants make their own food. They use water, sunlight, air, and chemicals in their leaves to make their own energy.

Every plant also has a way to **reproduce**, or make new plants. Some make sweet nectar to bring bees and butterflies, which **pollinate** the plant. Two giant plants put out a terrible smell to bring in flies and other meat-eating bugs to do that job. Redwoods and giant sequoias grow cones filled with seeds. Insects and fires help the cones open so that new trees can grow. Big or small, all plants have **adapted** to live in their special habitats.

Above: The corpse flower's stink draws flies and other bugs to pollinate the plant.

Giant plants grow around the world. Some, such as the giant sequoia, grow on mountainsides in California. Others, such as the mountain ash, grow on the mountainsides of Australia. Other giant plants, such as the corpse flower, grow well in rain forests.

Most of these giants grow only in their special habitats. Corpse flowers and *Rafflesia arnoldii* grow only in small parts of Indonesia. Giant sequoias grow in a small part of California. These places have the special things that allow these giant plants to grow.

Even with the right soil and the right amount of water, giant plants can only grow so big . Redwoods, ashes, and sequoias cannot pull water up to their treetops if they grow too tall.

Who Grows That?

Many people are interested in giant plants. People come from all over the country to see California's redwoods and giant sequoias. It would be hard to grow one of these trees in a greenhouse, though!

Other giant plants are not quite so big. Many **botanical gardens** grow the corpse flower and

Left: *Rafflesia arnoldii* is a rare flower. It grows only on the vine of another plant.

Rafflesia arnoldii, two stinky giant plants. They grow them so they can study them. They also grow them so people can see them since they grow in places that are hard to visit. Most importantly, they grow these plants to help keep them safe from **extinction**.

Above: The corpse flower is grown in botanical gardens. There the rare plant can be studied and viewed by people.

Giants in Trouble

Many giant plants are in danger of dying out. Luckily, people are working to protect them, or keep them safe. Redwoods and sequoias grow on protected land in the Giant Sequoia National Park and Redwood National Park, which are both in California. People are not allowed to cut trees in these places down.

The world's largest flower, *Rafflesia arnoldii*, is in trouble, too. These giant blooms grow in rain forests in Indonesia. The people there are not allowed to pick the flowers. The vine that this flower grows on is protected, too. Hopefully, these giant plants will be around to fascinate people for many years to come!

Above: Sequoia National Park is in California. It is famous for the giant sequoia trees that grow there.

The bark on a giant sequoia tree can be up to 3 feet (90 cm) thick at the base!

A Closer Look at the Giant Sequoia

Giant sequoias are not the tallest trees in the world. They are the most **massive** plants on Earth, though. The largest giant sequoia alive today is called General Sherman. This tree is 272 feet (83 m) tall. Its trunk is more than 30 feet (9 m) across and 109 feet (33 m) if you measure all the way around the outside of it.

Giant sequoias live only in a small part of the western Sierra Nevada in California. These trees grow on mountainsides that have dry summers and snowy winters.

Below: The General Sherman tree is a famous giant sequoia in Sequoia National Park. It is believed to be between 2,300 and 2,700 years old!

Above: Giant sequoias are not only huge, they can also live for a long time. The oldest known giant sequoia was guessed to be about 3,500 years old!

GENERAL SHERMAN

15

Meet the Corpse Flower

Titan arum is also known as the corpse flower. This is because its blooms smell like rotting meat. A full-grown bloom can be up to 12 feet (4 m) tall. Its powerful smell brings in bugs, which help pollinate the plant.

Once the bloom dies and the plant rests, a leaf begins to grow. The leaf can be up to 20 feet (6 m) tall. This leaf makes food for the **tuber** under the ground. This food will be stored in the tuber so it can grow a new flower the following year.

A Look at Mountain Ash

Eucalyptus regnans, or mountain ash, is one of the tallest trees in the world. It can grow to be more than 330 feet (100 m) tall. Mountain ash is native to Tasmania and Victoria, in Australia.

Mountain ash trees grow in cool, deep soil in mountainous places. They can live for about

400 years. The wood from mountain ash trees is prized for its use in building, furniture, paper, and flooring. It is also valuable to the environment. These trees are homes for many birds, such as the lyrebird and the wedge-tailed eagle. They are also home to mammals, such as the **endangered** Leadbeater's possum, and many insects.

Above: Birds such as the wedge-tailed eagle, shown here, make their homes in mountain ashes.

It can take many months for the bud of *Rafflesia arnoldii*, shown here, to bloom.

The World's Largest Flower

Plants have roots and grow in soil, right? This is true of many plants but not all of them. The plant with the world's largest flower does not grow in soil. It is a **parasite**. This parasitic plant is called *Rafflesia arnoldii*. It fixes itself to a vine called tetrastigma. It takes its food and water from this **host** plant.

Rafflesia arnoldii's flower can be 3 feet (1 m) across and it can weigh up to 15 pounds (7 kg). Like the corpse flower, *Rafflesia arnoldii* gives off the smell of rotting meat when it blooms. When flies and beetles come looking for food, they help pollinate the plant.

Below: Rafflesia arnoldii grows in the rain forests of Indonesia.

Below: This *Rafflesia arnoldii* bud is beginning to bloom.

1 The tuber of the corpse flower is huge. It can weigh up to 150 pounds (68 kg)!

2 *Rafflesia arnoldii* spends most of its life cycle unseen. When it is ready to reproduce, a bud forms and then grows into a flower.

3 *Rafflesia arnoldii* grows fruits that are eaten by squirrels and tree shrews.

4 The world's largest giant sequoia tree, General Sherman, weighs as much as 15 full-grown blue whales!

5 The wood from General Sherman would be enough to build around 26 houses!

It's a Fact!

6 *Titan arum's* leaf lasts for 9 to 12 months before it dies and a new one grows. New leaves grow every year. The plant blooms only every third year or so, though.

7 California redwoods, which are in the same family as giant sequoias, are taller than giant sequoias. Their trunks are not as thick, though.

8 A large giant sequoia can have about 11,000 cones that hold up to 400,000 seeds!

Glossary

adapted (uh-DAPT-ed) Changed to fit new conditions.

botanical gardens (buh-TA-nih-kul GAHR-denz) Gardens where special plants are grown and viewed.

endangered (in-DAYN-jerd) In danger of no longer living.

extinction (ek-STINGK-shun) The state of no longer existing.

host (HOHST) A living thing that supplies food for another living thing that lives on or in it.

massive (MA-siv) Having a very large mass.

parasite (PER-uh-syt) A living thing that lives in, on, or with another living thing.

pollinate (PAH-luh-nayt) To move pollen around to different plants, which helps them make seeds.

reproduce (ree-pruh-DOOS) To make more of something.

tuber (TOO-ber) A short, fleshy stem of a plant that generally grows underground.

Index

B
bugs, 7, 16

C
cones, 7, 22

F
flies, 7, 21

flower(s), 5, 8, 10, 13,
 16–17, 20–22

food, 6, 17, 20–21

G
giant sequoia(s), 7–8,
 10, 12, 14–15, 22

H
habitats, 7–8

height, 4

L
land, 5, 12

leaves, 6, 17, 22

R
redwood(s), 4, 7,
 10, 12, 22

S
seeds, 7, 22

smell(s), 5, 7, 16, 21

sunlight, 6

T
trunk(s), 5, 14, 22

Web Sites

Due to the changing nature of Internet links, PowerKids Press has developed an online list of Web sites related to the subject of this book. This site is updated regularly. Please use this link to access the list:
www.powerkidslinks.com/spe/giant/